THE HEART AS IT LIVED

Mansel Robinson

Playwrights Canada Press
Toronto • Canada

The Heart as it Lived © Mansel Robinson, 1997

Playwrights Canada Press is the publishing imprint of:
Playwrights Union of Canada
54 Wolseley Street, 2nd floor, Toronto, Ontario, M5T 1A5
Tel (416) 703-0201; Fax (416) 703-0059
E-mail: cdplays@interlog.com; Internet: www.puc.ca

Playwrights Canada Press operates with the generous assistance of The Canada Council for the Arts—Writing and Publishing Section, and the Ontario Arts Council—Literature Office.

Canadian Cataloguing in Publication Data

Robinson, Mansel, 1955–
The heart as it lived

A play.
ISBN 0-88754-554-8

I. Title

PS8585.O35168H42 1998   C812'.54   C98-930156-7
PR9199.3.R62H42   1998

Photo of Mansel Robinson: Ellen Moffat

First Edition: May 1998
Printed and bound in Canada

For my sisters

Verlie and Wendy

and in memory of Margaret Ann

I know without knowing how that the dead can remember
the movements of will, thought willing,
the gaze fixed at a distance that doesn't exist,
the mind in an endless war with itself—
those old cravings—but the striving to will themselves
from themselves is only a dream,
the dead know what death has brought is all they need now
because all else was already possessed,
all else was a part of the heart as it lived,
in what it had seen and suffered,
in the love it had hardly remarked coming upon it,
so taken it was with its work of volition.

From "The Covenant," by C. K. Williams

Mansel Robinson is a playwright and fiction writer. He has received the Saskatchewan Writers Guild Award for Drama, for *Collateral Damage* (Blizzard Publishing); the City of Regina Award for "The Heart As It Lived"; and the 1996 Geist Magazine Award for Distance Writing. Playwrights Canada Press published his first produced play, *Colonial Tongues*, in 1995, and Thistledown Press recently published his first book of short fiction, *Slag*. Mansel grew up in Chapleau, Ontario, and currently lives in Prince Albert, Saskatchewan.

Author's Introduction

I guess you could call this a history play: During the long Depression of the 1930s, thousands of single, young, unemployed men were sent to work camps run by the Department of Defence. They were paid twenty cents a day for their labour, and it was either that or starve. The government described these camps as voluntary. The men called them slave camps. I guess you could call this a history play, but the images in my head as I worked were of squeegee kids, squats, workfare, and bootcamps.

I guess you could call this a history play: In June 1935, hundreds of these young men boycotted the camps and began a journey now known as the "On To Ottawa Trek," an act of civil disobedience intended to confront the Bennett government with the demand for work and wages. The trek was halted by the government in Regina, and on July 1 mounted RCMP officers attacked a meeting of the men, sending dozens to hospital with gunshot wounds. I guess you could call this a history play, but the image I had pinned over my desk as I worked shows a young Nova Scotia fisherman confronting a riot squad in full regalia. The year is 1995.

I guess you could call this a political play: state and economic power, ideology, and the choosing of sides. I guess this is true. But the image in my head was of a young street survivor who's learned the lesson of his elders: compassion is for losers.

This is not the play I started writing. It's not even the play I *wanted* to write. I thought I had a story about history and redemption. But Annie and Zak had another story to tell, a story about greed, murder, larceny, and lies—a tender little tale of the 1990s.

Thanks to all the actors involved in the workshop and first productions, and especially to Glyn Thomas; Saskatchewan Arts Board; City of Regina; CBC Radio; Saskatchewan Federation of Labour; Sage Hill Writing Experience; Saskatchewan Playwrights Centre Spring Festival of New Plays; Reel Eye Media; Saskatchewan Archives; RCMP Museum; Kit Stratton; Bobby Jackson; Robert "Doc" Savage; Matt Shaw; Steve Brodie; Wayne Schmalz; Gordon McClellan; Rod MacIntyre; Patti Shedden; Rob Moffatt; Bob White; Ellen Moffat; Patrick MacIntyre for good talk and humour at the Henry VIII; and to John Murrell and Ben Henderson for keeping the wheels on.

Production History

The Heart as it Lived was first produced in Calgary at Alberta Theatre Projects' PanCanadian PlayRites '97 (D. Michael Dobbin, Producing Director), January 17 - March 2, with the following cast:

ANNIE	Sheila Paterson
ZAK	Christian Goutsis
FLO	Esther Purves-Smith
ZAKARCHUK	Edward Belanger
MITCHELL	Glyn Thomas

Director: Campbell Smith
Set Designer: Helen Jarvis
Costume Designer: Judith Bowden
Sound Designer: John Bent Jr.
Lighting Designer: Brian Pincott
Production Dramaturg: Rob Moffat
Design Assistant: Wes D. Pearce
Production Stage Manager: Dianne Goodman
Stage Manager: Colin McCracken
Assistant Stage Manager: Gina Moe

The play was subsequently produced at Theatre Network, Edmonton, February 24 - March 8, 1998, with the following cast:

ANNIE	Sharon Bakker
ZAK	Chris Fassbender
FLO	Shannon Quinn
ZAKARCHUK	Aaron Franks
MITCHELL	Patrick Howarth

Director: Ben Henderson
Production Designer: Robert Shannon
Composer and Sound Designer: Paul Morgan Donald
Stage Manager: Betty-Lou Hushlak

The Characters

ANNIE McBRIDE
In her mid-seventies. Walks with a cane she swings like an axe. Fifteen years old in the 1935 scenes.

ZAK
About twenty-two years old. Annie's great-nephew. On the road, scrawny, wears an old Oilers jersey, number 99.

FLO
About twenty years old in 1935. Annie's sister.

ZAKARCHUK
About twenty-two years old in 1935. Flo's boyfriend. Stocky build.

MITCHELL
About twenty-two years old in 1935. An RCMP officer. Wears a brown service uniform, rather than the red serge.

The Setting

A room, 10,000 books. June 1996. Regina, Saskatchewan.

Production Notes

Unless indicated (e.g. music bridge, blackout), scene follows scene without interruption. Some overlapping of scenes can be worked out in rehearsal. The "presences" of Flo and Zakarchuk come and go with the licence of shades. Like Mitchell, they are invisible to Zak.

I have included some of the stage business discovered in rehearsal for the first productions. Music bridges were not always used as indicated, and this seemed to work fine. Music in the first production included an instrumental version of "Hold the Fort," as well as several cuts from Ministry—Zak's preferred music.

Act One

Act One, Scene One

> *ANNIE stares at a package.*

ANNIE   "Meals on Wheels." Hunh. Turds on a trolley. *(throws package across the room)* I'd rather starve.

> *Blackout. Music bridge.*

Act One, Scene Two

> *A break-in is in progress. The beam of a flashlight bobs about in the darkness.*

ANNIE   Find what you're looking for?

> *ZAK locates ANNIE with the beam.*

ZAK   When I do, I'll let you know.

ANNIE   The police will be here in about thirty seconds, boy. If I were you I'd start running.

ZAK   Is that right?

ANNIE   That's right.

ZAK   Pretty quick response time. What, you got e-mail to a donut shop?

ANNIE   Twenty seconds.

ZAK   How ya doin' Annie?

ANNIE   And I'd start running empty-handed—you'll make better time.

ZAK   I asked you how ya doing, Mizz McBride.

ANNIE   About fifteen seconds. Go.

ZAK   I know your name.

ANNIE   So you research the people you rob. I'm not impressed.

ZAK   I know all about you.

ANNIE   Ten seconds.

ZAK   You were a teacher.

ANNIE   Tell it to the police.

ZAK   You never got married.

ANNIE   No wedding rings for you to steal, that's right.

ZAK   But you had a boyfriend.

ANNIE   Most women have a boyfriend. These days most men have one, too. Go.

ZAK   He died.

ANNIE   The cops are seconds away.

ZAK   The government murdered him.

Pause.

ANNIE   Who are you?

ZAK   I'm family.

ANNIE   I have no family.

ZAK   You got me.

                      Pause. ANNIE turns on the light.
                      Pause.

ANNIE   You're a Zakarchuck. Aren't you.

ZAK   My friends call me Zak.

ANNIE   You're not friend, you're not family—get that
                      straight.

ZAK   So where's the cops? It's way past thirty seconds.
                      (pause) You didn't call them, did you. *(pause)*
                      Shouldn't bluff like that, Annie. It's like pointing
                      an empty gun at a stranger. You could get hurt.

ANNIE   Thanks for the advice. Now what do you want?

ZAK   It's not a crime to visit long lost relatives, is it?

ANNIE   *What* are you doing here?

ZAK   I'm glad you asked about the family. Things aren't
                      going too well.

ANNIE   I don't care.

ZAK   Dad's in jail. Not a pretty story. Some politician
                      wants to ship cons to Mexico. Tryna saves money
                      or something. Sure hope they don't rent Dad to the
                      Mexicans, he's dumb enough in English. *(pause)*
                      My Mom? Oh, she left a long time ago.
                      Whereabouts unknown.

ANNIE   None of this matters to me.

                      Pause.

ZAK   Wanna hear about Flo?

ANNIE   No.

ZAK   Favourite sister. Only sister.

ANNIE	Ancient history.
ZAK	Granny had an accident last month.
ANNIE	Flo wasn't born stupid but she caught on soon enough.
ZAK	Choked to death.
ANNIE	Finally bit off more than she could chew did she?
ZAK	Choked to death on food-bank tuna.
ANNIE	So much for charity.
ZAK	You ever eat food-bank tuna?
ANNIE	I'm a vegetarian.
ZAK	*(smiles)* No. You sound more like a carnivore.
ANNIE	Oh. You want me to be nice. *Fine*, I'm *nice*. Tell me about yourself. You got a girl?
ZAK	Not just now.
ANNIE	Why not? You just get out of jail? You look like you just got out of jail. Pretty white around the gills.
ZAK	No jail.
ANNIE	Then what have you been doing with your life?
ZAK	Whatever I have to.
ANNIE	Are you still in school?
ZAK	No.
ANNIE	How far did you get?
ZAK	Out.

ANNIE	Too much for you.
ZAK	Slowing me down.
ANNIE	Slowing down your trip to the bottom of the barrel?
ZAK	*(smiles)* I'm not going to the bottom. I can promise you that.
ANNIE	My guess is you're already half way there.
ZAK	No big deal. Just a rough patch of Zakarchuk luck.
ANNIE	Poor boy. Times are tough.
ZAK	Not for you. Look at this place. Antiques. A million books. Not bad for tough times.
ANNIE	I see where this is headed.
ZAK	Do you?
ANNIE	You want money. Forget it.
ZAK	I'm taking care of business.
ANNIE	Unemployed, aren't you.
ZAK	Half the planet's unemployed, Annie. It's not a sin to be out of a job.
ANNIE	Not a sin, no. Close though. *(pause)* Well. Thanks for bringing me up to date on the family news. I imagine you have to be on your way now. Taking care of business. Good night. Goodbye.
ZAK	It's kind of late.
ANNIE	I know that.
ZAK	I'm travelling by thumb. *(waits)* Not much traffic this time of night. *(waits)* It's cold out there by the side of the road.

ANNIE	You break into my house, now you want a place to sleep?
ZAK	I didn't break in.
ANNIE	Pawing through my things.
ZAK	I was just waiting for you.
ANNIE	You didn't knock.
ZAK	I guess you didn't hear me.
ANNIE	Some bum in the middle of the night.
ZAK	Family.
ANNIE	A stranger.
ZAK	Your sister's grandkid.
ANNIE	Is that what she taught you? The government killed Mitchell?
ZAK	Yeah. One night. Maybe two.
ANNIE	He was killed by thugs.
ZAK	Thugs, government—same thing. You won't even know I'm here.
ANNIE	Thugs like that Zakarchuk.

FLO *enters.*

ZAK	Ancient history, right? Can I stay?
ANNIE	They shoulda strung him up until his eyeballs blew.
ZAK	Are you listening to me?
ANNIE	No.

ZAK	C'mon, Annie.
ANNIE	Go away.
ZAK	I want a place to stay.
ANNIE	There's a hotel in town.
ZAK	I don't have any money.
ANNIE	Get a job.
ZAK	It's the middle of the night.
ANNIE	Get a night job.
FLO	Last chance, little sister.

ANNIE *looks at her. Pause.*

ANNIE	*(quiet)* Go away.
ZAK	Annie. I'm hungry.
ANNIE	You're a pitiful thing. Young and strong, and on the bum, not a dime to your name. Begging from an old woman.
ZAK	Just pretend I'm the grandson you never had.
ANNIE	I don't like children.
ZAK	You were a teacher.
ANNIE	What's that got to do with liking children?
ZAK	*(smiles)* OK. You want the truth?
ANNIE	I want you gone.
ZAK	Flo didn't have much to leave in her will. Big surprise. All there was was one little request. She said to come here. She said to deliver a message.

ANNIE	Then deliver it and get out of my house.
ZAK	That's the weird part. She didn't tell me what it was.
ANNIE	Don't you lie to me.
ZAK	Telling you straight. She didn't tell me the message. Other thing, she told me not to leave, no matter what you said. *(short pause)* So, here I am. *(short pause, grins)* I think you inherited me.
ANNIE	I don't want you.
ZAK	I'm all she had.
ANNIE	I don't like you.
ZAK	Times are tough—take what you get.
FLO	Last chance, little sister.

Pause.

ANNIE	She sent you here?
ZAK	Weird, eh?
ANNIE	Not so weird. She makes the mess, I get to clean it up.
ZAK	Can I stay?

ANNIE *pauses, looks at* FLO.

ANNIE	If I help out, you'll leave me alone?
ZAK	Deal.

She turns back to ZAK.

ANNIE	You start work at 7 a.m.
ZAK	I didn't ask for a job.

ANNIE   Work, yes—a four-letter word is it? Tough. Here's the deal—in Coles Notes, just to make it easy for you. There's chores around the place. Cleaning and dusting. Women's work. I'll pay you by the hour, minimum wage, deduct for room and board. Rule number one: I make the rules. Take it or leave it. Welfare is for losers.

ZAK   Nice try, Annie. But I'll take it. *(grins)* Food in the fridge? Don't move. I can find it. I can find anything I want. In any house I want.

ANNIE   My God, what a botched job you are.

ZAK   You don't even know me.

ANNIE   I know who you come from.

ZAK   Yeah, well, forget about her. I'm here. Deal with me.

ZAK exits. It is 1935.

FLO   Last chance, little sister.

Pause.

ANNIE   Go away, Flo.

FLO   "Go away, Flo." That's all you have to say to me? *(pause)* Daddy's throwing me out. But I guess you know that. Aren't you even going to ask me where I'm going?

ANNIE   A home for whores, for all I care.

FLO   Something's happened to you, Annie.

ANNIE   Mitchell happened to me. Mitchell.

FLO   Not just Mitchell. Something else. Something not very pretty. I don't know what it is. But when I figure it out, I'm gonna let you know.

ANNIE	Don't you have to pack?
FLO	I was wrong. You're not some naive little school girl—not even close.
ANNIE	Go. You and your bastard. Go.
FLO	OK, Annie. If that's your choice. Not sisters. Strangers. No goodbyes. Silence.

FLO exits.

| ZAK | *(offstage)* Annie. We're outta peanut butter. |

ANNIE *nods thoughtfully, looking in FLO's direction.*

| ANNIE | *(to herself)* Uh huh. Catastrophe. |

Music bridge.

Act One, Scene Three

ANNIE *is alone.*

| ANNIE | So. I guess that's what I have to do. Work the boy. Cut him off at the knees. It's what he needs. What she should have taught. Values. Hnh. The teacher's nightmare—no one breeds but the unfit. |

ANNIE *hears a noise behind her.* ZAK *is casing the room, pocketing some antique knick-knack.*

Mitchell? *(turns)* You. You're supposed to be working.

| ZAK | On a break. |
| ANNIE | I want this house spic and span. |

ZAK   Easy, mon. Slow and easy, mon. No hurry, no worry, mon. Just a leetle break, mon.

ANNIE   Trouble with this country. Everyone lazy as a bureaucrat.

ZAK   Ask you a question?

ANNIE   No.

ZAK   Did you know you talk to yourself?

ANNIE   I don't talk to myself.

ZAK   OK. Mutter.

ANNIE   I *don't* talk to myself.

ZAK   Now that I'm living here, you might as well talk to me.

ANNIE   You don't live here, you work here.

ZAK   C'mon. I'm trying to establish a, a, a, relationship.

ANNIE   A relationship?

ZAK   Yeah. You know. Based on, uh, mutual, uh, affection.

ANNIE   I told you once—I don't like you.

ZAK   I grow on people.

ANNIE   So do boils.

ZAK   *(smiles)* Whaddya say? Friends?

ANNIE   Your break's over.

> ZAK *is at a bookshelf. He flips through a book, assesses it.*

ZAK   One more question?

ANNIE	No.
ZAK	These are worth money, aren't they.

Pause. She looks at him.

ANNIE	You keep your grubby paws where they belong.
ZAK	You know, you could sell all this stuff. House, too. Move to Jamaica, mon. Live in the sunshine, mon. Lie on the beach. Hang out 'til you drop like an old coconut. You should think about it. Beats living in Saskatchewan-awanna-wanna-wanna die anywhere but here.

Pause.

ANNIE	Jamaica, eh?
ZAK	No more winter.
ANNIE	Hmn. Good for the bones. Maybe that's not such a bad idea. Oh, I'd need help, though. Someone to carry the luggage. Fetch the suntan oil. You want a job, come with me?
ZAK	You kidding me?
ANNIE	Hah. Ripped your leg right off, didn't I? Just looking for a free lunch.
ZAK	Not a free lunch.
ANNIE	What, then?
ZAK	I consider this an opportunity.
ANNIE	For what?
ZAK	Who knows. That's what makes it an opportunity.
ANNIE	You might learn something?
ZAK	Maybe.

ANNIE	You might get something?
ZAK	Bonus.
ANNIE	You might escape something. You might be hiding here.

Pause.

ZAK	That's right. I'm lying low.
ANNIE	I knew it.
ZAK	Yup. A big-time criminal.
ANNIE	I knew it.
ZAK	Executed two nuns and a cocker spaniel. So be careful. I'm dangerous.
ANNIE	If you want your pay, you'll get back to work.
ZAK	Pay me decent money, and I'll contract out.
ANNIE	Now.

They look at each other.

ZAK	That's OK. I can only stand old people for so long. *(puts book away)* Nice books. Real nice.

ZAK exits.

ANNIE	Hnh. Contract out. Surprise surprise—he's got a brain. Potential. Surprise surprise.

FLO has entered. It is 1935.

FLO	You don't eat. You don't sleep. How long do you think you can live like that?
ANNIE	What do you care?
FLO	I care.

ANNIE	You care about yourself.
FLO	I'm sorry. I'm sorry about Mitchell. When I dragged you out of the house that night, when I dragged you downtown, I didn't know. I was only worried about Zakarchuk. I didn't know what happened to Mitchell. I'm sorry.
ANNIE	What am I gonna do with sorry?
FLO	I just want to hold you. I want you to hold me. That's all. Comfort. I know how you feel. If anyone knows, I know. And you need me here.
ANNIE	I don't need you here. I don't want you here.
FLO	I need you. I've needed you for weeks. *(ANNIE is silent)* I've missed you.
ANNIE	Can't help you.
FLO	Look at us. We've both lost someone. We're on the same side of that. We're not apart. We're together. *(silence)* Let's not lose each other, too. *(silence)* I didn't do this, Annie. Neither did Zakarchuk.
ANNIE	Who did, then?
FLO	I don't know. But he didn't hurt you. He didn't hurt me. He was like a light, you know. Just a light in all this ugliness. He talked about possibilities, the future, things getting better. He didn't talk about killing.

Pause.

(simply) And now he's gone. Maybe they've put him on a boat somewhere. And languages he doesn't understand, and puke and sweat and pissing where he sleeps. Then maybe he's kneeling in a line with twenty other guys on frozen ground in a country he doesn't even remember. And the pistol shots are coming up the line. One guy at a time.

ANNIE   Times are tough.

FLO   You aren't that hard.

ANNIE   Don't tell me what I am.

Pause.

FLO   If this was a test, we've failed. *(gets set to leave)* I think I'm going to have a child.

ANNIE   I hope you do. I hope it kills you.

This registers. FLO leaves. ANNIE returns to the present.

Tooth for a tooth. Isn't that the way? Did I invent that—no. No. Was I cruel? Cruel was losing you, that was cruel. Did we ask for that—no. No. That day. Of all days, that day, just cruel. Annie M., you said. A slip of a girl, the rings of Saturn. A silly boy. A silly, beautiful boy. And I was going to be, Annie Maud McBride, will you, yes... yes....

FLO has entered. It is 1935.

FLO   Where were you?

ANNIE   Flo?

FLO   Where were you?

ANNIE   Jeez, you look awful.

FLO   Where were you?

ANNIE   What's that smell?

FLO   It's piss.

ANNIE   What?

FLO   You were supposed to meet me at the baseball game. Where were you?

ANNIE   I had a headache so I stayed home.

FLO   Doing *what*?

ANNIE   What happened, Flo?

FLO   Doing what?

ANNIE   Reading. A book. Stephen Leacock. Are you going
               to tell me what happened or not?

FLO   How come you didn't come out tonight? Dominion
               Day celebrations, all that crap.

ANNIE   It's a free country. I can stay home to read if I
               want.

FLO   Don't make me puke.

ANNIE   Are you drunk or something?

FLO   He told you, didn't he?

ANNIE   Who told me what?

FLO   He told you they were going to smash them.

ANNIE   Speak English or I'm going back to sleep.

FLO   I left the ball game. I went to a meeting. And the
               reason you stayed home is 'cause Mitchell told you
               the cops were going to smash that meeting.

ANNIE   I don't know what you're talking about.

FLO   Baseball bats. Guns. Horses. And Mitchell told you
               not to leave the house. But you didn't tell me.

ANNIE   He knows you're going around with the enemy,
               he's not gonna tell—

FLO   Zakarchuk isn't the enemy—he's just a guy. And
               he's been missing for hours. He might even be
               dead.

ANNIE   Daddy warned you, didn't he. He warned you about those guys.

FLO   Get dressed. We're going out.

ANNIE   I'm not going anywhere.

FLO   Get *dressed.*

ANNIE   I'll call Daddy.

> FLO *grabs* ANNIE.

FLO   You wake anybody up and I promise you I'll strangle you before they get to this room.

ANNIE   OK, Flo. OK.

FLO   Enemy, eh? Let's go see the battlefield.

ANNIE   Where are we going?

FLO   You like downtown. We're going downtown.

ANNIE   In the middle of the night?

FLO   Special night, Annie. Happy birthday, Canada.

ANNIE   Why are you doing this?

FLO   I want you to see what happened while you were home reading *Sunshine Sketches of a Little Town.*

> *Quick lighting change. Downtown Regina. Night.*

FLO   OK. What do you smell?

ANNIE   Nothing.

FLO   Work at it.

ANNIE   Something weird. I don't know what it is.

FLO	It's tear gas. What else?
ANNIE	The air. The wind.
FLO	Whisky.
ANNIE	You're nuts.
FLO	A policeman runs up to me. He yells at me. Breaths whisky in my face. He swings his baseball bat. He misses me. I run up the alley.
ANNIE	You've lost your marbles.
FLO	There's a horse coming at me, nearly on top of me. I run up another alley. And when I'm safe, I realize I've soiled myself. I smell that.
ANNIE	Why would they chase you?
FLO	Because I was here.
ANNIE	That doesn't make any sense.
FLO	Doesn't it?
ANNIE	No.
FLO	Whipped down dogs don't fight back.
ANNIE	That doesn't happen here, Flo.
FLO	Annie. It's happening. Are you blind?
ANNIE	Can we go home now?
FLO	You go. I can't find Zakarchuk. I'm going to check the hospitals again.
ANNIE	Come on home. Have a hot bath.

FLO	Why, do I stink?
ANNIE	It's over. Just let him go. Where ever he is, just let him go.
FLO	I thought we were sisters, friends.
ANNIE	We are.
FLO	You're telling me he's nothing.

Pause.

ANNIE	He's not one of us.

Pause.

FLO	What do you see here?
ANNIE	I don't want to do this anymore.
FLO	What do you see here?
ANNIE	Smashed windows. Smashed automobiles. A mess.
FLO	Smashed dreams—do you see those? Smashed hope?
ANNIE	No.
FLO	Then imagine yourself, the things you want: to own a house with rose bushes and hummingbirds. Now imagine *me*, snug in my room with a good book and my door locked, while you get the piss beat out of you by a cop. Think about it, Annie.

FLO starts to leave.

ANNIE	You're just making speeches, Flo.

FLO	No. This time it's not a speech. Not somebody else's words. This time the words are all mine.

FLO exits.

ANNIE	Flo. Come home. Please. Flo.

ANNIE follows her, still in 1935.

Music bridge.

Act One, Scene Four

ZAK enters. He tosses down his work gloves, wipes the sweat off his forehead, and stretches out on the floor.

ZAK	Nut bustin' old cripple. Christ, Christ, Christ.
ANNIE	*(offstage)* What was that?
ZAK	Uh. Crickets. I said there's too many crickets in this stupid province.
ANNIE	That curse just cost you an hour's wage.
ZAK	I said "crickets."
ANNIE	Lying about it makes it two hours.
ZAK	C'mon, Annie.
ANNIE	Rule number one—
ZAK	Alright. Alright.

ZAK lies on the floor, exhausted. ANNIE enters. She pokes him with her cane.

ANNIE	What's the matter with you?
ZAK	I'm sore all over. I have blisters all over. I have heartburn. I have a headache. I have muscle spasms. I quit.
ANNIE	You can't quit. With all your coffee breaks, sick days, and sleeping in— *(checks a little black notebook)* I estimate you've done eight hours work. Deducting board and room and all those fines— looks like you owe me three hundred and change. Would you like an itemized bill?
ZAK	Kill me. Sell my skeleton to a medical school. You'll make a good buck.
ANNIE	That's illegal.
ZAK	I won't press charges. I promise.
ANNIE	Hunh. *(she sits and watches him)* You come from a lazy generation, you know that, don't you.
ZAK	Yeah. It's the war.
ANNIE	What war?
ZAK	The war against the young.
ANNIE	Good Lord. The war against the young?
ZAK	Cops hate us. Teachers hate us. You all hate us.
ANNIE	We've given you everything.
ZAK	The hospitals are full of old folks like you drooling in their soup and peeing their beds. When I get sick I might as well go die on the street 'cause the only thing you got for the young are abortion clinics.
ANNIE	As social studies that fails with flying colours.

ZAK   Sitting in here with the curtains closed, what do
               you know about what's going on out there? No
               radio, no TV. A bunch of dusty old books can't tell
               you nothing about dodging landlords in the middle
               of the night....

ANNIE   Then pay your bills.

ZAK   And dodging cops....

ANNIE   Then obey the law.

ZAK   Going hungry....

ANNIE   Then get a job. I've worked all my life.

ZAK   I work, too.

ANNIE   You can barely get out of bed before lunch.

ZAK   Since I was fourteen.

ANNIE   A paper route. Big deal.

ZAK   You know how a fourteen-year-old makes his
               living these days? *(makes a crude gesture)* With his
               mouth, in the front seat of a car.

ANNIE   *(turns away)* I don't know what you're talking
               about.

ZAK   You can keep your eyes closed. But the world still
               turns and shit still happens.

ANNIE   Another five dollars.

ZAK   I came here hungry with eight cents in my pocket.
               What do you call that?

ANNIE   Your own fault.

ZAK	Yeah. I can see why you live alone.
ANNIE	I live alone because a gang of immigrant butchers stole what—

> *She stops, the words and thoughts suddenly gone. ZAK observes her, waiting.*

ZAK	You OK?

> *Pause.*

ANNIE	*(gathers herself)* I don't know what happened to you, boy, but your excuses sound familiar.
ZAK	They're not excuses.
ANNIE	I've heard it all before. The Crash of '29. Soup kitchens.
ZAK	I don't need to hear this, it's got nothing to do with me.
ANNIE	It has everything to do with you. Lots of us toughed out those hard years, lots of us. But all we hear is the whining, and the belly-aching, and the lying—"battlefields" and "baseball bats" and, and, "whipped down dogs." The propaganda of thugs like that Zakarchuk.
ZAK	Don't tell me—never knew the guy.
ANNIE	You're just like him. Blaming other people for your problems. And I find that pathetic. Not surprising, given the name you carry. But pathetic just the same.
ZAK	Be nice to me, Annie.
ANNIE	I am being nice to you.
ZAK	Be *nicer*.

Pause.

ANNIE   Alright. Let's change the deal.

ZAK   Your deals suck.

                ANNIE *hobbles towards the books.*

ANNIE   I'm going to pay you to sit on your bum.

ZAK   Cool.

                She takes an old diary off the shelf.

ANNIE   I'm going to pay you to sit on your bum and read this.

ZAK   What is it?

ANNIE   It's my diary. It's about me and Mitchell. The one you think the government murdered. It's about that time.

ZAK   Why?

ANNIE   Because I'm a teacher. Because you're a mixed-up kid on his way to the bottom. Because Flo and that Zakarchuk are sending you to the bottom. Because unless you see that, the bottom is all you'll ever see. You've heard their version too long.

ZAK   Annie. Listen to me? I don't *have* a version.

ANNIE   Where do you think this "war against the young" comes from? You believe their propaganda.

ZAK   I believe what I see.

ANNIE   That Zakarchuk—

ZAK   Grampa. Grampa. What are we talking about Grampa for?

ANNIE   Is that what she taught you to call him? Grampa?

ZAK	So what?
ANNIE	Your father was a bastard. You're not entitled to call his old man "Grampa."
ZAK	Bastards run in this family. So do bitches.
ANNIE	That'll be five dollars.
ZAK	"Bitch" is in the dictionary.
ANNIE	What do you know about dictionaries?
ZAK	Nothin'. But I'm learning lots about bitches.

Pause. ANNIE *almost smiles.*

ANNIE	I wasn't always a bitch.
ZAK	'Course not. Everybody's gotta sleep.

She does smile.

ANNIE	Will you read it?

He takes the diary and flips a few pages.

ZAK	You're going to pay me to read?
ANNIE	But you have to read it aloud. I don't trust you.
ZAK	*(shrugs)* Beats digging.

FLO *and* ZAKARCHUK *have entered.*
It is 1935.

FLO	I'm scared.
ZAKARCHUK	So am I.
FLO	You're not supposed to say that. You're supposed to tell me that everything will be fine. That everything will work out, that no one will be hurt.

ZAKARCHUK	If they want blood, blood's gonna come.
FLO	Don't say that.
ZAKARCHUK	Cops do what cops do. Ask those miners at Bienfait. 'Course, you'll need a Ouija board to talk to them. *(makes a "whoo" ghost sound)*
FLO	Lie to me.
ZAKARCHUK	There's enough lies already.
FLO	I want to be ignorant.
ZAKARCHUK	You'll watch, Flo. You're gonna watch and remember.
FLO	No. I don't want to know.
ZAKARCHUK	Flo. The cops train with machine guns. They're not even cops anymore. They're soldiers. On your pretty little streets. In your pretty little town. Soldiers. With bayonets. Right point, left point, butt to the groin, long point, right breast. *(he "bayonets" her with his hand, not touching her)* Bayonets.
FLO	I'm scared. I—
ZAKARCHUK	You listen to me. I need you. I'm just a dirty immigrant to these people, barely human. My story doesn't count. But you. With your grandfather's house. Your... "McBride," your lovely British name. Your... place... in the community, a schoolteacher. You'll watch. You'll learn. You'll speak. It's your job. Do it. *(pause)* Or if I end up with a bullet in the back of my neck, are you even gonna notice? Just one more bohunk buried in a wheat field.

Pause.

FLO	*(quiet)* You're cruel.

ZAKARCHUK	*(quiet)* I'm a criminal, aren't I? A communist thug. What do you expect.
FLO	I'm frightened. That doesn't mean I'm a—cop.
ZAKARCHUK	Then why do you make their goddamn job so goddamn easy?
FLO	I am not making—
ZAKARCHUK	I know what I see.
FLO	But you don't know me.
ZAKARCHUK	You believe a used shirt donated to some bohunk equals justice. You believe a couple of school-teacher fairy tales will close the camps. You—
FLO	Is that what you think? I'm naive? Charity is useless? Teaching kids is useless? Fists and boots are better? We have nothing in common? Is that what you think?
ZAKARCHUK	I don't have time to be gentle with you.
FLO	Then what's the point? Of anything you say? Of anything you believe. No *time* to be gentle? I don't know who you are right now.
ZAKARCHUK	Then listen.
FLO	I have *been* listening.

Pause.

ZAKARCHUK	My father disappeared. *(pause)* I was a kid. *(pause)* He was at the strike in Winnipeg. My mother figures he was picked up the night the strike was broken. She doesn't know for sure. But we never saw him after that. If the cops put him on a boat. He was a socialist. If they put him on a boat back to the Ukraine, then the Russians would have killed him. The only thing the Russians hate worse than a capitalist—it's a socialist.

Pause.

ZAKARCHUK   I can't do any more jail. The next time they put me in a little stone room—I'm gonna splash my brains all over the walls. *(pause)* I'm scared of heights. *(pause)* I'm scared of dogs. *(pause)* I never been with a woman. *(pause)* And I don't swim in rivers, 'cause of the fish.

Pause.

FLO   Alright. A deal. Knowledge. *(kisses him)* For knowledge.

They exit. ZAK *reads aloud from* ANNIE*'s diary. He's not the best reader in the class.*

ZAK   "I haven't seen much of Mitchell these last few days. He's been busy keeping an eye on the on-to-Ottawa boys. Of course, that's not what Mitchell calls them. Something about inbred foreigners...." Oh oh, Annie. Sounds like your boyfriend was some kinda skin-head.

FLO enters.

ANNIE   I don't remember it that way.

ZAK   "These criminals won't be here forever, Mitchell says. But I should keep away, because there might be trouble. So I keep away from them. I wish Flo would keep away too...."

FLO *steps forward. It is 1935.*

FLO   You sicked Daddy on me. Didn't you.

ANNIE   I didn't sic him on you.

FLO   He knows about Zakarchuk. About my plans for the fall. Everything.

ANNIE   I'm trying to protect you.

FLO   From what?

ANNIE   It's not our fight. Whatever problems those guys got, it's not our fight.

FLO   The school board pays me in pig slop.

ANNIE   It's better than nothing. Times are tough.

FLO   Don't be such a schoolgirl, Annie.

ANNIE   There's a law, Flo. I read it in the paper. You're not supposed to give them food, you're not supposed to give them money. Nothing. You could go to jail.

FLO   Boy, that's some law. I wouldn't want your boyfriend's conscience when he has to enforce that one.

ANNIE   It's the law.

FLO   There's police in town from all over the place. They need that many cops to arrest people making sandwiches for hungry boys?

ANNIE   It's the law.

FLO   Or do you think they're here to help celebrate Dominion Day?

ANNIE   Then why doesn't your boyfriend leave? Get back on the freights the way he got here.

FLO   They won't let them back on the freights. They even closed the highway.

ANNIE   Then he should've stayed where he was.

FLO   Jesus, Annie.

ANNIE   Don't swear at me.

FLO	Then don't be so stupid.
ANNIE	I am not stupid.
FLO	I like him. And I'm scared for him.
ANNIE	Then help him sneak away.
	Pause.
FLO	He won't do it.
ANNIE	See? His own fault.
FLO	I said he should sneak away, and I'd meet him when he was safe. He laughed. He said "Safe to what? Safe to go hungry? Safe to lick the policeman's boot? There's no safe left." *(pause)* I'm scared, Annie.
ANNIE	This'll all pass. The newspapers say good times are just around the corner.
FLO	Oh, well, then. We'll just have to wait. *(she waits impatiently)* Are the good times here yet?
	FLO *exits.* ANNIE *returns to the present.* ZAK *is flipping through the pages of the diary.*
ZAK	You're probably going to test me on this.
ANNIE	Probably.
ZAK	Keep it simple, OK? Like, multiple choice?
ANNIE	A bum. Or a citizen. That's your choice.

> ZAK *is at a new page. He smiles and reads aloud:*

ZAK
"Bored again. Bored. Bored. Bored. I sit in class and watch my fingernails grow. Mrs. Beatty stands at the front, swaying from foot to foot like a tired cow, mooing, moo moo moo about something or other, chewing her cud. I wish I could sleep with my eyes open. She's too slow to catch on, and school would be useful for a change, a place to dream...."

ANNIE
That's called humour, boy.

ZAK
School too much for you?

ANNIE
Pick another passage.

ZAK
I like this one.

ANNIE
Then you're through for the day.

ZAK
Cool.

> *He exits, mooing.*

> FLO *and* ZAKARCHUK *have entered. It is 1935.*

FLO
Take off your shirt.

ZAKARCHUK
(stripping quickly) That's the best offer I've had in months.

> FLO *runs her finger slowly from his nipple to belt buckle.* ANNIE *watches with discomfort.* FLO *hands* ZAKARCHUK *a new shirt.*

FLO
You'd better put this on.

ZAKARCHUK
Why?

FLO
You'll catch a cold.

ZAKARCHUK   It's eighty degrees.

FLO   You'll catch a summer cold.

ZAKARCHUK   You really want me to get dressed?

> FLO *runs her finger from his belt buckle to his other nipple.*

ANNIE   Tramp.

> ANNIE *exits.*

FLO   For now.

ZAKARCHUK   *(smiles)* Yeah. I like you.

FLO   I like you.

> *They look at each other for a moment longer. Then he moves away to put on the shirt.*

ZAKARCHUK   Summer cold, eh?

FLO   The worst kind.

ZAKARCHUK   Where'd you get this?

FLO   I stole it from a guy.

ZAKARCHUK   He's gonna miss it.

FLO   Doubt it. He's got about a million of 'em.

ZAKARCHUK   You're gonna get yourself in trouble.

FLO   Watch me shiver.

> *He finishes tucking in the shirt.*

ZAKARCHUK   Nice shirt.

FLO   Nice body.

ZAKARCHUK	*(smiles)* Bold as brass, girl.
FLO	You scared of me?
ZAKARCHUK	Watch me shiver.

> *They exit.*
>
> *Music bridge.*

Act One, Scene Five

> ANNIE *chases* ZAK *in. She is using a walker instead of her cane.*

ANNIE	You little pig. (ZAK *snorts like a hog)* You think it's funny?
ZAK	I think you're funny.
ANNIE	Dirty little pig.
ZAK	A natural act of nature.
ANNIE	My foot.
ZAK	I couldn't help it.
ANNIE	You urinated, in my garden. Like a pig. Like a dog.
ZAK	Watering the turnips, big deal.
ANNIE	Rose bushes.
ZAK	Whatever.
ANNIE	I won second prize one year.
ZAK	Maybe now you'll win first.

ANNIE	Vulgarity. Did she teach you that, too? How about smut? Did she teach you smut? And lechery?
ZAK	You're awfully excited about a little—
ANNIE	*(measured)* I am not excited. I am disturbed. I am perturbed. Do you know the meaning of that word? Perturbed?
ZAK	What's the matter Annie, it's just—
ANNIE	*(measured)* It's not what's the matter. It's who's the matter.
ZAK	I read your dull diary. I clean your dirt. I do the deal. What are you complaining about?
ANNIE	The deal was if I helped out, you'd leave.
ZAK	You haven't finished helping me yet.
ANNIE	I am not a social worker. I am not a criminologist. I am not a psychiatrist, or a priest, or a miracle worker. I'm just a teacher. But you don't want to learn. Maybe we should just forget the whole thing. Maybe you should just go.
ZAK	I can't.
ANNIE	Four doors in this house lead outside. Pick one.
ZAK	I'm the messenger.
ANNIE	With no message.
ZAK	Maybe it's in code. Yeah, a puzzle, a mystery, a, a, cryptic. Whaddya think, Annie, in behind those... cataracts of yours, in behind those milky old eyes, you got a mystery pinballin' around: Why'd that crazy old bat send him here?

I like mysteries. I mean, this ain't a great mystery, just two old bats—Ozzie Ozborne, bats in the belfry—two old bats duking it out, sister on sister, counter punch and run. So go ahead. Boot me out—and kiss off your answer to the mystery.

ANNIE   I already have my answer. Coles Notes—she sent you here to show how wrong she was. You are the shining example of her failure. You—are an apology.

ZAK   No. I'm a shining example of success.

ANNIE   You?

ZAK   Me. Some people get all twitched up with that history crap. But history was yesterday, and yesterday doesn't exist. Just like hockey. Gretzky keeps his eye on the play coming up. Starts thinking about what happened thirty seconds ago, he'll be picking a cross-check out of his skull. Only one game in town—the next ten seconds. And that's how I play, Annie—the next ten seconds.

ANNIE   Cheap philosophy.

ZAK   Survival.

ANNIE   Is that all that counts?

ZAK   Isn't it?

Pause.

ANNIE   Yes.

ZAK   *(grins)* See? Success.

Pause.

ANNIE   What about your dead?

ZAK   My what?

ANNIE	They're everywhere.
ZAK	I have no dead.
ANNIE	What about Flo?
ZAK	I don't talk. About Flo. End of discussion.

ZAK exits. ANNIE watches him go.

ANNIE "I have no dead." What a lucky boy. Survival. Yes. A head on his shoulders, give him that. Rude as a monkey, but he knows what's necessary. What did she want? Me down there with her, stinking wet with urine? What good would that do? None. Stay away. Like you said, stay away. And keep my mouth—shut. She wants a confession? I confess. At fifteen I knew where I stood. She wants a confession? I confess. At fifteen I chose—survival. End of discussion.

FLO has entered. It is 1935.

FLO	Annie. Are you awake?
ANNIE	Flo? Yeah. What time is it?
FLO	Late.
ANNIE	Daddy's gonna tan your hide.
FLO	I'm in love.
ANNIE	Are you crazy?
FLO	Yes.
ANNIE	Already?
FLO	It doesn't take long with the right guy. I got goose bumps all over.
ANNIE	You're cold.

FLO	You don't know anything about love, do you.
ANNIE	You're cold. C'mon. Get into bed. C'mon. I'll warm you up.

> FLO *sits beside* ANNIE. *They cuddle together.*

ANNIE	Just like old times, eh?
FLO	Yeah.
ANNIE	When we'd talk all night.
FLO	Catch hell in the morning for snoozing in the porridge.
ANNIE	Yeah.
FLO	Nights I tickled your back 'til you fell asleep.
ANNIE	Yeah.
FLO	The good old days.

> *They enjoy the closeness for a moment.*

ANNIE	You love this hobo?
FLO	He's not a hobo.
ANNIE	Whatever. You love him?
FLO	I think so. He's really interesting. He's been everywhere. The Yukon. Cape Breton. He's been to *Montreal*, Annie. *Montreal*.
ANNIE	Daddy's gonna have a conniption.
FLO	Daddy.
ANNIE	He is.
FLO	Daddy's a fraud.

ANNIE	Flo.
FLO	He walks around downtown like some kind of big shot. But Grampa made the money. All Daddy has to do is spend it.
ANNIE	That's not fair.
FLO	And scratch Grampa's ass when it itches.
ANNIE	What's the matter with you?
FLO	But Daddy's gonna help my friend out. Gonna give him a brand new dress shirt. I'll have to steal it out of his drawer first. But Daddy won't mind, he's a big shot. *(ANNIE hides her head)* I work, Annie. I work hard the whole school year, and at the end of every month they pay me in carrots. That's all a teacher's worth these days. Carrots. So I have to live at home in the summer, and everybody pities me. I don't want pity. And I'm worth more than carrots. *(pause)* Keep a secret?
ANNIE	I don't like your secrets anymore.
FLO	When I go back teaching in the fall, I'm not just going back teaching. I'm gonna talk to everyone in the district, all the teachers who get slopped like pigs instead of paid like people. And then we're gonna tell the school board that our work is important. And we want to be treated like human beings again.
ANNIE	Don't do it, Flo.
FLO	Why not?
ANNIE	We're not those kind of people.
FLO	What kind of people are we?
ANNIE	The kind that don't act like that.

FLO	If I don't, I'm just a coward. And all I'm teaching those kids is how to be cowards, too.
ANNIE	Teach them geography. Teach them Greek. Don't do it, Flo.
FLO	*(gently)* Oh, Annie. *(shakes her head)* You go back to sleep, now. *(pause)* Are you still seeing Mitchell?
ANNIE	Sure.
FLO	You be careful with that one.
ANNIE	He's a nice guy, Flo.
FLO	Just be careful. That's all.

> FLO *exits.* ANNIE *returns to the present.*

ANNIE	Careful. No. A good boy. *(pause)* A lesson. Yes.

> *Music bridge.*

Act One, Scene Six

> ZAK *enters, holding up a few two-dollar bills.*

ZAK	What's this?
ANNIE	It's payday.
ZAK	This?
ANNIE	Yes.
ZAK	These are twos.

ANNIE	I'm not blind.
ZAK	Are you kidding me?
ANNIE	I don't kid about money.
ZAK	No shit—make a nickel scream, you.
ANNIE	That's five more dollars.
ZAK	Take some more. 'Cause I'm gonna use some adult language. I'm gonna say you're a blood-sucking bitch of a miser.
ANNIE	It's time you learned the value of a dollar.
ZAK	We had a deal.
ANNIE	I'm sticking to the deal.
ZAK	With old two-dollar bills?
ANNIE	It's what you're worth. It's not my fault. And maybe it's not your fault either. Maybe it's just Flo.
ZAK	I don't talk about Flo.
ANNIE	So let's talk about Mitchell. That's who you needed when you were growing up. Mitchell. He'd have taught you, he'd have turned you into a citizen.

ZAK *rolls his eyes, here it comes again.*

You talked about war. He was in a real war, he fought on the side of people who work hard at their jobs, who save their money, who make a home for themselves with the labour of their hands. The war was fought not too far from here. Twelfth Avenue. Osler Street and South Railway. Market Square and Victoria Park.

ANNIE   Angry men shouting slogans. Lead pipes in their
             hands like clubs. A policeman. He's twenty-two.
             He's a handsome, happy boy, and his name is
             Mitchell. And he has the guts and gumption to
             stand up to the criminals on Scarth Street and say:
             "Enough. You're hungry? Go to work. You're
             poor? Get a job. You have it tough? Get busy. No
             more blackmail. No more taking what others have
             earned. Enough."

             Breaking glass, whistles, shouts, gunshots. The
             smack of steel on a skull, the cheers as a policeman
             goes down. The mob cheers as Mitchell goes down.
             He reaches out with his left hand. He disappears in
             the mob. Hands with iron bars raised to the sky.
             The clubs crash down, they're raised again and
             again and again and again. And then there is
             silence, and then there is stillness. And then there
             is nothing. And then there is nothing. And then
             there is nothing.

                          Pause.

ZAK   We have better riots after the Stanley Cup.

ANNIE   That morning, Mitchell had asked me to marry
             him. I was too young. "I'll wait," he said. "I'll
             wait." I said yes. It was Dominion Day, 1935. I
             was fifteen years old. *(pause)* As it turns out, it's
             me who does the waiting. He returns to me. One
             day a year. Every year. It's our life together. It's
             my marriage. And last year was our diamond
             anniversary.

                          Pause.

ZAK   This dead cop visits you?

ANNIE   He has a name. Mitchell.

ZAK   What's he look like?

ANNIE   Like himself.

ZAK	Can he fly?
ANNIE	Television.
ZAK	Does he?
ANNIE	No.
ZAK	And he's a ghost.
ANNIE	He just is. He was alive. Now he's something else—spirit of the time, spirit of the place. I don't care. He is.
ZAK	This is too weird.
ANNIE	You have a lot to learn about this world.
ZAK	He visits you.
ANNIE	Yes.
ZAK	This is too weird.
ANNIE	He could have taught you.
ZAK	It's either Alzheimer's, or there's some kind spell on you. Whoooo, whoooo.
ANNIE	Television and welfare.

> ZAK *cavorts about, whoo whoo whooing.*

ANNIE	The twin forks of the dev... of the...

> *The words are gone again.* ANNIE *looks at the money, and speaks in a distant voice:*

Don't spend it... one place... the... pennies, take care of them... waste not, want... not....

> *She is very quietly having a stroke. She looks at the money, doesn't recognize it; it falls out of her hand. ZAK observes her intently.*

ZAK   Annie. Annie? Annie.

> *ZAK doesn't know what to do. He checks her pulse, still doesn't know what to do. He pockets the money, still doesn't know what to do. So he proceeds to rob her—books, jewelry, anything.*
>
> MITCHELL *enters.*

MITCHELL   Hustler. Profligate. Hooligan. Delinquent. Culprit. Fraud. Swindler. Hoodlum. Hood. Crook. Felon. Convict. Vandal. Bohunk.

> *ZAK exits with the loot. As he goes,* MITCHELL *reads "The Riot Act."*

MITCHELL   "A riot is a an unlawful assembly that has begun to disturb the peace tumultuously. His Majesty the King charges and commands all persons being assembled immediately to disperse and peaceably to depart to their habitations or to their lawful business, upon the pain of being guilty of an offence for which, upon conviction, they may be sentenced to imprisonment for life. God save the King...."

> *Blackout.*
>
> *End of Act One.*

Act Two

Act Two, Scene One

ANNIE *sits in a wheelchair. She is
motionless, staring.* ZAK *stands beside
her.*

ZAK *invaded* ANNIE's *world in Act
One, and now he's taking over. He's
brought his CD player into the room,
and has made himself comfortable. He
works hard to get a reaction from her,
by blasting music in her ear, etc. Then
he kills the music, stands beside her,
and tries blowing in her ear. He blows
in one ear, with his hand at her other
ear, wafting about as if his breath is
blowing through an empty skull. He
tries something else, then something
else, but there is no reaction at all.
Finally, he pulls out a handgun and
points it at her, threatens her. He aims
it at her face and pulls the trigger. It's a
water pistol.*

ANNIE *sits motionless for a long
moment. Finally, she slowly raises her
hand and wipes the water from her face.*

ZAK   *(smiles)* Physiotherapy.

ZAK *exits.*

Blackout. Music bridge.

Act Two, Scene Two

> ANNIE *in her wheelchair, recovering.*
> *She has the money, so she sits in the*
> *Cadillac of chairs: electric, well padded,*
> *with pouches, saddle bags, chrome, and*
> *class. She is learning to drive it. It is*
> *not going well, but when she finally*
> *gets the hang of it, she is pleased with*
> *herself.*
>
> *Blackout. Music bridge.*

Act Two, Scene Three

> ANNIE *in her wheelchair.* MITCHELL
> *is with her, and stays onstage for the*
> *rest of the play.*

ANNIE   I'm dying. (MITCHELL *touches her face, to*
comfort her) Knowing it's coming, knowing it's
sitting just inside my skull. One breath. One
hiccup. And it's over. I've buried so many people.
But it's my turn now. And I'm not ready.

MITCHELL   Tell me what you need.

ANNIE   I was ready. I think I was ready. Then the boy
opens the door, and he doesn't close it behind him.

> *Pause.*

MITCHELL   Hello, Annie M. Sweetheart of a day, isn't it? The
kind of day you want to save in your pocket and
not haul out 'til February.

ANNIE   *(gently)* Not yet, Mitchell.

MITCHELL   I don't know much about much, Annie M., but I
             think we could use those words right about now.

ANNIE   I don't want your comfort.

             Pause.

MITCHELL   The year your father died. And when your mother
             went. Even in those hard years, Annie M., you
             wanted comfort.

ANNIE   I want it. But it's not what I need. Not right now.
             I'm thinking.

MITCHELL   *(waits)* Yes?

ANNIE   I'm thinking... *(she pauses, then turns and smiles)*
             ...that you still look the same. The same as last
             year. And the year before that.

MITCHELL   My condition has its advantages.

ANNIE   Yes.

MITCHELL   I still have my hair.

ANNIE   And your teeth.

MITCHELL   Yes.

ANNIE   And your figure. I wish I had mine.

MITCHELL   You look lovely, Annie.

ANNIE   You might have your teeth, but you need glasses.

MITCHELL   It's not like you to fish for compliments.

ANNIE   You try getting old.

MITCHELL   There's nothing I would have liked more.

             Pause.

ANNIE	I know. *(pause)* I'm sorry, Mitchell.
MITCHELL	Pretty women never need to apologize.
ANNIE	You must work hard on your flattery.
MITCHELL	I don't have to work.
ANNIE	What do you see when you look at me like that?
MITCHELL	You.
ANNIE	Gray and dry as an old shoe.
MITCHELL	I see a yellow dress drying in the sun, glowing in the sunshine. A dress lighter than sunshine, dancing in the wind. I see you on a July morning, looking better than any July morning I remember.
ANNIE	Are you making fun of me?
MITCHELL	I see you, Annie. Because from the first time I did see you, I never saw anyone else.

Pause.

ANNIE	April Barnes?
MITCHELL	April? Beef to the heels.
ANNIE	Ethel James?
MITCHELL	No.
ANNIE	She was a beautiful girl.
MITCHELL	Ethel changed boyfriends faster than prairie weather.
ANNIE	She scared you.
MITCHELL	The Force doesn't care for fast girls.

> *ANNIE does a little turn with her wheelchair.*

ANNIE   You'll have no trouble with me, then.

> *They both smile.*

MITCHELL   Fix the lights, Annie.

> *Pause.*

ANNIE   Flo's trying to tell me something.

MITCHELL   And I'm trying to give you something.

ANNIE   I'm intrigued by it all. Like a wreck on the highway. I don't want to look. But I do. I look. Bodies everywhere. I look.

MITCHELL   Then look at me, Annie M. Face me.

ANNIE   I do face you, Mitchell. Every year.

MITCHELL   Forget the kid. Forget your sister. All you have to do is fix the lights.

ANNIE   *(smiles)* You are a persistent boy, aren't you.

MITCHELL   Isn't that why you like me?

> *ANNIE fixes the lights. It is a bright, sunny day, July 1, 1935. MITCHELL takes a short stroll, a cop on his beat.*

MITCHELL   Hello, Annie M. Sweetheart of a day, isn't it? The kind of day you want to save in your pocket and not haul out 'til February. We could use a day like this in February, a little bird-song and sunshine in the middle of winter, be as sweet as a honeymoon.

ANNIE   And what do you know about honeymoons?

MITCHELL   Nothing, yet.

ANNIE   You getting married?

MITCHELL   Hope so.

ANNIE   Who to?

MITCHELL   Pretty girl.

ANNIE   What's her name?

MITCHELL   Agnes... Audrey... Antionette... something like
                  that.

ANNIE   Mustn't care for her too much, if you don't even
                  remember her name.

MITCHELL   *(snaps his fingers)* Annie. That's it. Annie.

ANNIE   I know her. She's too young for you.

MITCHELL   I'll wait.

ANNIE   How long?

MITCHELL   Three years. Four. I don't care. I'll wait.

ANNIE   What if she changes?

MITCHELL   She'll only get better.

ANNIE   What if she gets a big pimply nose, and her hair
                  goes frizzy?

MITCHELL   I'll keep my eyes closed.

ANNIE   What if she gets TB, or the Spanish Influenza?

MITCHELL   I'll buy the best doctors in Saskatchewan.

ANNIE   Then she becomes a nag and a shrew.

MITCHELL   I'll make her too happy to nag.

ANNIE	And she refuses to cook.
MITCHELL	Then I'll learn to cook.
ANNIE	And she hates your mother.
MITCHELL	No problem. I hate my mother.
ANNIE	You do not.
MITCHELL	I will if you ask me.
ANNIE	I think you're lying.
MITCHELL	The ends justify the means.

Pause.

ANNIE	Do you love this Annie?
MITCHELL	The first time I saw her, down at Wascana creek. Just a slip of a girl but the sun in her hair gave her a halo like the rings of Saturn.
ANNIE	My sister warned me about sweet-talkers.
MITCHELL	*(smiles)* I want some goodness in my life. All I see all day are drunks and thieves and trouble makers. Christmas Day. Dominion Day. All I see is the dirt people do. But when I come home at the end of the day, when I come home to you, all that'll disappear. I want some goodness in my life. I want you. It's that simple. Annie Maud McBride. Will you marry me?

> ANNIE *is reaching towards* MITCHELL. *Before she can say yes, before the moment can continue,* ZAK *enters. He is wearing a New York Rangers jersey, number 99, and is stuffing himself with pizza. He sees* ANNIE *reaching out to the empty air. He stops.*

ZAK	Annie?
ANNIE	Go away.
ZAK	Are you having another seizure?
ANNIE	I said go away.
ZAK	The way you're sitting. You look like you're having another seizure.
ANNIE	I'm talking to Mitchell. Leave me alone.
ZAK	I think maybe I should call an ambulance.
ANNIE	I don't need an ambulance.
ANNIE	Annie. Ghosts don't exist.
ZAK	He's here. And I'm tired of you, and I'm sick of them, and I have some business with Mitchell.
ZAK	I better stick around.
ANNIE	Please. Not today. Not today.
ZAK	Ghosts are dangerous. Hollywood says so.
ANNIE	Hollywood has nothing to do with it.
ZAK	OK, we're making progress. It's not Hollywood. It's chemical. Or electrical. Either way, your brain is wearing out. I'm sticking around. You might need someone to call a hearse.
ANNIE	What I need is Mitchell.
ZAK	Or better yet, maybe I should talk to this guy. Hey. Horse cop. You hear me? Dead guy. Wanna hear something funny? We sold you guys to Disney. You guys are cartoons now. Royal Canadian Mounted... P-P-P-Porky Pigs. Actually that's not Disney, but—

ANNIE   Go away.

ZAK   I wanna tell Porky a story. 'Bout one of his
buddies. *(talks directly to* ANNIE*)* Hear me, Porky?
This cop. This cop busts me for a B 'n' E. I'm
only fourteen, so he offers me a deal: Front seat of
the cruiser, take the law into my own mouth,
problem solved. What are you gonna do? Times are
tough. After that he picks me up two three times a
week, go for a ride—and pays me good money
when the ride's done. Beats boosting and the hours
are better.

One day he says to me, no warning, that I'm too
old. Steady pay, Porky, good steady pay—all of a
sudden I'm too old at fifteen. But I'm thinking on
my feet, I make him an offer. I say I'll become his
supplier. I know what he wants, how he wants it.
Customer satisfaction guaranteed. Couple days later
I supply him a pink-cheeked little kid with a great
little ass. It's Hollywood, happily ever after. Cop
get his jollies, the kid makes his rent, I got a new
improved career. Ready steady the world turns
smooth.

ANNIE   You disgust me.

ZAK   Don't start, Annie. Don't disappoint me now. This
is the world you lived in, it's the world you're
gonna die in. No fairy tales. No bullshit. Nothing
but the next thirty seconds. Are you with me here?
No Mitchell. No ghosts.

                      ANNIE *drives away from him.*

We gotta remember the kind of place we live in.
It's the only way. Like, you pay me wages—right?
But you don't pay me what I need. I need more. So
I take more. Real world, Annie. Survival. Nothing
else counts. You know that. So I been selling your
books. Cash. Colour TV. VCR. CD player. See?
We shoulda gone to Jamaica.

ANNIE	What are you?
ZAK	I'm blood.
ANNIE	You're nothing, a criminal.
ZAK	Yeah, and you're a thief—so what?
ANNIE	I never stole a thing in my life.
ZAK	You lie to your judge, and I lie to mine—let's not lie to each other.
ANNIE	I am a not a thief.
ZAK	You're slipping again. Real world. Where'd you get this house?
ANNIE	My father gave it to me.
ZAK	And Flo got what?
ANNIE	She left. Her choice.
ZAK	She got nothing.
ANNIE	The rest I worked for.

Pause.

ZAK   (*like a bored teacher reciting a tired lesson*) The Zakarchuks—in Coles Notes, just to make it easy for you. Flo's knocked up, kicked out of the house, hits the road. Dad born—a single mom sixty years ago, that must've been shit. Dad hustling by the time he's twelve, Flo goin' apeshit 'cause he's a dumb little thief, always getting caught. And Flo's got no backup, 'cause Grampa's long gone on some boat to nobody knows where.

And Flo's a loser. Fighting slumlords half the
night, fightin' scumbag minimum-wage bosses all
day, getting nowhere. A loser. Years and years and
years of Flo playin' loser but she won't take two
bucks of my daddy's hustled money. And my daddy
still ain't too bright so he knocks up some bar-
stool junkie. And Flo ends up taking care of that
bouncing baby boy. And I'm hustling by the time
I'm ten. I'm a fast-mouthed little hustler and I
hardly ever get caught. And more years and years of
Flo playin' loser but she won't take two loonies of
my hustled money either. And then, surprise,
surprise: Flo the loser dies the way all losers die.

So here's the mid-term test, Annie. Are you a
loser? Yes or no?

And I'll be in my room watching movies. And if
you blow another head-pipe, get Mickey Mitchell
Mouse to phone for a body-bag.

> ZAK *exits.* FLO *and* ZAKARCHUK
> *have entered. It is 1935.*
>
> ZAKARCHUK *sits in a chair.*

ZAKARCHUK   Alright, teacher. Teach me.

FLO   What do you want to know?

ZAKARCHUK   I want to know about you.

FLO   I like my work. I like my kids. I worry about
them, where they're going to end up. And who
they'll be when they get there.

ZAKARCHUK   You a good teacher?

FLO   Yes.

ZAKARCHUK   What's your best lesson?

FLO   The Golden Rule.

ZAKARCHUK   I think you mean The Rule of Gold.

>*FLO circles him.*

FLO   I warn them against a game that they're going to learn as they get older. They'll learn that the world is a game of musical chairs. That they must rush around as the music plays, and when the music stops, they must fight for a chair. And that the losers must stand outside the game, ashamed. And that the winners can sit in their overstuffed chairs and gloat.

ZAKARCHUK   Yeah. That's the game alright.

FLO   Doesn't have to be that way.

ZAKARCHUK   So, how do you play?

FLO   I just say that there are enough chairs to go around. *(stands in front of him, hikes up her skirt)* I figure all we have to do is work out more *(straddling his lap)* imaginative seating arrangements.

>*FLO hesitates, then kisses him on the cheek. She gets up.*

ZAKARCHUCK   Any rules for that game?

FLO   Just one. No losers.

>*She exits. He follows. ANNIE watches them leave.*

ANNIE   In the middle of the summer, she'd chop forty sticks of kindling. She was ten or twelve. She'd stick the kindling in the ground, in lovely straight rows, in the backyard. And she'd stand at the front of her classroom. And she'd teach. The Lord's Prayer. The names of flowers. Clouds.

MITCHELL	She taught a lie, Annie. There are no imaginative seating arrangements. I wish there were.

Pause.

ANNIE	Compare and contrast. My life, in Coles Notes: I lose Mitchell. I do not wither. I do not fold. I finish my schooling. I graduate from loneliness. I pass into solitude. A year is a click on an abacus. Twenty years. Forty. Sixty. I define family, I define love—just fancy words for scar tissue. My world grows smaller: The size of a room. The size of a fist. On a quiet night in June, a good book and silence, the door opens. The floor shakes slightly. Unnoticeable, really. Just a tremor under the skin of the earth that sets the tea-cup to rattling in its saucer.

Pause.

MITCHELL	You've changed.
ANNIE	No. People don't change. Not really. I'm just unsettled, that's all. Unsettled.
MITCHELL	I've seen you unsettled. This is different.
ANNIE	I've no say in the matter. She's got me thinking.
MITCHELL	Listen to me. Please. You're wasting your time. Alright? Just rooting around in... old muck.
ANNIE	Yes. Muck to the hub-caps.

Pause.

MITCHELL	Is that what you want?
ANNIE	It's what I've got.

Pause.

MITCHELL   One day a year, Annie, we have a moment that
             shines like Venus in the morning sky. I know, I
             know—more sweet-talk. But one day a year, we
             have something untouched by the world.

                         He holds up an engagement ring.
                         Pause.

ANNIE   The world's here, Mitchell.

                         Pause.

MITCHELL   Do you want me to leave?

                         Pause.

ANNIE   No.

                         Pause.

MITCHELL   So what happens now?

                         Pause.

ANNIE   I don't know. I guess I have to wait.

                         Pause.

MITCHELL   Alright. We wait.

                         Pause.

ANNIE   Thank you, Mitchell.

                         He kisses her.

                         Music bridge.

Act Two, Scene Four

> ZAK *hobbles in, using* ANNIE*'s walker.*

ZAK   *(looking around)* Dead guy around? *(*ANNIE *ignores him)* I guess I scared him off.

ANNIE   He isn't scared of you.

> *Pause.*

ZAK   I was thinking. Maybe I made a mistake about him.

> *Pause.*

ANNIE   A mistake?

ZAK   Yeah.

> *Pause.*

ANNIE   About Mitchell?

ZAK   Yeah.

> *Pause.*

ANNIE   What kind of mistake?

ZAK   I was thinking I shoulda used his magic powers to get the dishes done.

> ANNIE *turns away, disgusted with herself.*

ANNIE   The dishes are your job.

> ZAK *tours the room with the walker.*

ZAK	Actually, what I was really thinking is now that we're partners, we should hire somebody to do the house cleaning.
ANNIE	Partners?
ZAK	Yeah. A crew. The, the, the, the ghosts. Yeah. Invisible thieves. Whatddya think?
ANNIE	*(looks at him)* Let me guess. On top of everything else, you're a dope fiend. Partners.
ZAK	Partners in crime.

Pause. She watches him tour the room.

ANNIE	Are you in here for a particular reason? Come to steal the rest of my books?
ZAK	Just ridin' the range. Mendin' fences. Checkin' the property. Our property. Keepin' 'er safe for the family. Bad people out there, Annie. The triads and the gang-bangers come swarmin' in here, you wouldn't stand a chance without me.

Pause.

ANNIE	Have you ever been in a mental institution?
ZAK	Yup.
ANNIE	I thought so.
ZAK	In there quite a while, too.
ANNIE	Did they let you out, or did you escape?
ZAK	Oh, can't get out, Annie. Born into it. Called livin'. One whacked-out planet you guys built.
ANNIE	And what have you built?
ZAK	Absolutely nothing. I just cruise around in your wreckage. I kinda like it.

Pause.

ANNIE   You know what, boy?

ZAK   What's that, Annie?

ANNIE   You're full of shit.

ZAK laughs, and stops.

ZAK   That'll be five dollars. I'll mark it down.

ZAK exits, and on his way out scoops her little black book.

FLO and ZAKARCHUK have entered. It is 1935.

FLO   *(practising his name)* Zaki— Zakachuk. *(gets it right)* Zakarchuk.

ZAKARCHUK   What's the matter, never met a bohunk before?

FLO   Don't talk like that.

ZAKARCHUK   I've been called worse.

FLO   Not by me.

ZAKARCHUK   You'll be called things, too, keep walking around with me.

FLO   Free country.

ZAKARCHUK   Is it?

Pause.

FLO   When you do have a job, what do you do?

ZAKARCHUK   Carpenter when I can. Ran booze for Sam Bronfman one time. Jackass of all trades I guess. How about you?

FLO	I'm a teacher.
ZAKARCHUK	Teacher. Shoulda known.
FLO	What's wrong with teaching?
ZAKARCHUK	Yes ma'am, no ma'am. Two times two is take your orders from the boss man. The kings and queens of Europe, and the Irish famine wasn't murder, just an act of God. Is that what you teach?
FLO	I teach what I know.
ZAKARCHUK	You teach what you've been taught.
FLO	If you don't like me—you don't have to be here.

Pause.

ZAKARCHUK	I'm not very good talking to people like you. I'm sorry.
FLO	You can trust me.
ZAKARCHUK	Friend of mine. Came to Canada when he was four. They blackballed him out of the camps for agitation then they put him on a boat. I only been here since I was five. There's people want to put me on a boat for some country I only heard about in books. Trust? Big word.

Pause.

FLO	My sister goes around with a mounted policeman. You should know that.
ZAKARCHUK	Oh, boy, do I know how to pick 'em.
FLO	I picked you. *(he looks at her; pause)* That first day when you all marched into town. I picked you.
ZAKARCHUK	Why me?
FLO	You have secrets. I have secrets.

ZAKARCHUK   *(smiles; pause)* Your sister. She like that guy?

FLO   I think they're thinking about getting married.

ZAKARCHUK   You like your sister?

FLO   Of course.

ZAKARCHUK   You protect her?

FLO   She's my sister.

ZAKARCHUK   Tell her this Mountie, he's gonna need permission
              from his commanding officer to marry her. Tell her
              it ain't the communists who nationalized women—
              the RCMP beat them to it. Tell her that's what
              kind of guy she's going around with.

FLO   Are you making this up?

ZAKARCHUK   A man follows those kind of orders I wouldn't let
              anywhere near my sister.

FLO   He's just a kid himself.

ZAKARCHUK   An iron heeled, goddamn Cossack.

FLO   A farm boy with no farm to work.

ZAKARCHUK   So how come some of us with no farms to work
              choose not to join the Cossacks?

FLO   I don't know.

                            Pause.

ZAKARCHUK   Me neither, teacher. A mystery.

                            They exit. ANNIE *returns to the
                            present. Pause.*

ANNIE   Did I know that, Mitchell? Did I forget?

MITCHELL	It doesn't matter.
ANNIE	It doesn't?
MITCHELL	I'm here.
ANNIE	They tell you who to marry?

Pause.

MITCHELL	No. We ask.
ANNIE	You had to ask about me?
MITCHELL	Yes.
ANNIE	Before you talked to me?
MITCHELL	Yes.
ANNIE	Why?
MITCHELL	Orders. Rules. It makes no difference. They said yes to you.

Pause.

ANNIE	Was I your first choice?
MITCHELL	Drop it, Annie.
ANNIE	I thought you were going to see me through this.
MITCHELL	But I didn't say I'd like it.
ANNIE	Was I your first choice?

Pause.

MITCHELL	No.

Pause.

ANNIE   Who was?

                                Pause.
MITCHELL   Ethel.

                                Pause.

ANNIE   Ethel. You said you didn't like fast girls.

MITCHELL   The Force doesn't like fast girls.

ANNIE   You would have married her?

MITCHELL   I don't know.

ANNIE   You would have married her?

MITCHELL   Yes.

ANNIE   So you do like fast girls.

MITCHELL   I'm here, Annie.

ANNIE   What if they had said no to me? *(pause)* Mitchell?

                                Pause.

MITCHELL   I follow orders.

                                Pause.

ANNIE   I see.

MITCHELL   It was my job.

ANNIE   It's OK, Mitchell. It's OK. I see, that's all. I see.

                        Music bridge.

Act Two, Scene Five

                    ZAK *shuffles cards, a Vegas pro.*
                    ANNIE *watches for a time.*

ZAK   Wanna play?

ANNIE   You'd only cheat.

ZAK   Everybody cheats. You know that. *(ZAK plays in silence)* Oh yeah. Some bills came in the mail. I need access to one of your bank accounts.

ANNIE   Say that again?

ZAK   I need into your account to pay some bills.

ANNIE   I know what you said. I just wanted to hear it again. I need the laugh.

ZAK   You think it's funny.

ANNIE   Side-splitting.

ZAK   They cut off your lights you won't think it's funny.

ANNIE   I already see more than I want to see, boy.

ZAK   Don't worry about it. I'm pretty resourceful. Wouldn't want a fine upstanding professional old thief like yourself ending up on the street, now, would we?

                    Pause.

ANNIE   Did anyone anywhere at any time actually like you?

                    Pause.

ZAK   Flo did.

ANNIE   Yeah, well, Flo. *(pause)* Are you sure she liked
               you? Are you sure she just didn't *love* you—not
               like you, but *love* you, in spite of your thieving
               and lying, and your back-chat, and your sneer—are
               you sure she didn't just love you, you little thug,
               with some hair-brained Christian love, because Flo
               was some kind of *saint*?

               He looks at her, and smiles.

ZAK   Don't be jealous, Annie. I like you the best. Mean
               as cat shit. I wish *you* were my grandmother.

               ZAK *plays in silence.*

ANNIE   Have you kidnapped me?

ZAK   I thought about it.

               Pause.

ANNIE   And?

ZAK   Everybody's dead. Nobody around to make the
               ransom.

ANNIE   Then rob me now and get it over with.

ZAK   But I like it here. We're good for each other.

ANNIE   You won't get a cent. I'll die first.

ZAK   Then you'll still be twitching on the living room
               floor, barely starting to cool, and I'll be down at
               the nearest bank machine draining your long life
               dry. You gotta love the technological revolution,
               Annie. PIN numbers. Debit cards. Makes robbery
               so civilized. *(he shows her the little black book)*
               And when forgetful old people have to write their
               numbers down—piece of cake.

ANNIE   You're an evil thing.

ZAK   Don't use such big words. I'm illiterate, remember.

> *He blows her a kiss, then exits.*

ANNIE   Evil. Evil.

> FLO *and* ZAKARCHUK *have entered.*
> *It is 1935.*

ZAKARCHUK   It's pretty funny if you think about it.

FLO   I don't think it's funny.

ZAKARCHUK   Sure it is. They slop us grey meat in the camps, right? Some upstanding citizen sells this garbage to the government for about five-hundred percent profit. Then this citizen writes his member of Parliament screaming about the bums on relief stealing from the taxpayer.

> FLO *isn't smiling.*

C'mon, Flo. That's called irony. OK, OK. You'll like this part. The reason I'm in a friggin' slave camp in the first place is 'cause I live in a country where the only guys workin' steady are the undertakers.

> FLO *still doesn't smile.*

OK. One more. They pay me twenty cents a day, right? So near as I can figure, I can retire in about—six thousand years.

> *Looks at* FLO.

What's the matter, Flo? You got no sense of humour?

FLO   I wake afraid in the morning, I fall asleep afraid, in a narrow bunk also sold to the government at five-hundred percent profit. I live afraid I will die in a boxcar somewhere, that I will never do work that I love, that I will never love a woman and hold our child.

FLO   I look at the cracked mirror in the bunkhouse and, with the smell of old socks and armpits up my nose, I see another day gone for good. And I am old and wasted and forgotten, and I am twenty-two years old.

           Pause.

ZAKARCHUK What are you up to, girl?

FLO   I wanted to be you for a second. That's called empathy.

ZAKARCHUK I didn't hear you laughing.

FLO   'Cause I don't think you *are* laughing.

ZAKARCHUK I still don't get what you're up to.

FLO   Facts we ignore. Feelings we don't forget.

ZAKARCHUK Then you forgot something important. I'm riding to Ottawa to tell those gentlemen that I'm still kicking and I want my future back. Nothing more. Nothing less. And nothing's gonna stop me, girl. Nothing.

FLO   OK. I'll feel that, too.

           Pause.

ZAKARCHUK You're different. Aren't you.

FLO   I don't know.

ZAKARCHUK You are.

FLO   I'm just me.

ZAKARCHUK How'd you get to be you?

FLO   When I was four, I was struck by lightning.

ZAKARCHUK	*(smiles)* So where did you learn... empathy? Your people?
FLO	No, they hate boys like you.
ZAKARCHUK	Like me?
FLO	Reds.
ZAKARCHUK	What makes you think I'm a Red?
FLO	If someone sold me for twenty cents a day, I'd be Red *(snaps her fingers)* like that.
ZAKARCHUK	*(smiles)* You got a boyfriend?
FLO	You got a girlfriend?
ZAKARCHUK	You want a boyfriend?
FLO	You know any my type?
ZAKARCHUK	What's your type?
FLO	Someone with imagination. Someone with heart.
ZAKARCHUK	Think you'll find him?
FLO	What do you think?
ZAKARCHUK	There might be a guy. Twenty-thousand railroad miles. Been in the kalaboose couple times. Do any kind of work 'cept kick a stone-broke family into the street. I know a guy who thinks the present is bullshit but imagines some other kind of future. How about somebody like that?
FLO	Sounds like an interesting guy.
ZAKARCHUK	You could do worse.
FLO	Good looking?
ZAKARCHUK	Blind woman on a galloping horse'd think so.

FLO	I don't have a horse.
ZAKARCHUK	So close your eyes.

> FLO *smiles. They look at each other for a moment.*

FLO	This guy. Was he really in jail?
ZAKARCHUK	Would that scare you?
FLO	Should it?
ZAKARCHUK	Scare easily?
FLO	Is he dangerous?
ZAKARCHUK	To who?

> *Pause.*

FLO	I guess I'll have to take my chances.
ZAKARCHUK	I like a girl who takes chances.

> *Pause.*

FLO	Are you hungry?
ZAKARCHUK	I ate this morning.
FLO	You're starvin', aren't you?
ZAKARCHUK	Most of the time.
FLO	Let's go see what Granny's got on the stove.
ZAKARCHUK	Granny hates people like me.
FLO	Perfect.

> *They exit.* ANNIE *has driven her wheelchair towards them. She watches as they leave.*

ANNIE	Look at them. They sparkle. Like... Christmas lights.
MITCHELL	Christmas lights, Annie?
ANNIE	Yes.
MITCHELL	They were doomed. This country hates dreamers, you've known that your whole life.
ANNIE	They sparkle. *(pause)* Do we?
MITCHELL	One day a year. It's what we've got.

Pause.

ANNIE	Were we capable of love?

Pause.

MITCHELL	We are what we are.
ANNIE	You don't have any regrets, do you?
MITCHELL	Regrets? And then what? Atonement? And then what? Redemption? It doesn't work that way.

Pause.

ANNIE	Our wedding night. What do you imagine it would have been like? Ecstasy or disaster? What do you think?
MITCHELL	I think women don't talk about such things.
ANNIE	Some things haven't changed since '35, but some things have: Women say what they want. Tell me what you think.
MITCHELL	No.
ANNIE	Tell me.
MITCHELL	I don't take orders from women.

ANNIE   Disaster: What is this thing you show me, what
                 does it do, where does it go, it hurts, this whole
                 event is ridiculous, no wonder people do it in the
                 dark.

MITCHELL   Are you going to leave us with nothing?

ANNIE   Ecstasy: I take you in my hand, in my mouth, in
                 my body. You tell me the skin inside my body
                 feels like nothing else on earth, smooth, and wet,
                 and warm, and tight—it's a gift for you I carry in
                 my hips.

MITCHELL   Stop it.

ANNIE   Disaster: I rise out of myself and watch from the
                 dimness above: A grunting dog and his obedient
                 bitch. Copulation. Fornication. Propagation. You
                 grunt. And grunt again. And sleep quickly. I listen
                 to the ticking of the clock. Your seed draining from
                 me, growing cold. You turn over and fart in your
                 sleep.

MITCHELL   Good God, Annie.

ANNIE   Ecstasy: My fingers claw across your back, across
                 your thighs, across your buttocks, your fingers in
                 my mouth, in all of me, everywhere, your tongue
                 everywhere, your tongue searches me everywhere,
                 you lick me like a cat, I purr like a cat, so well and
                 so imaginatively licked, I purr like a cat into sleep.

                 Pause.

MITCHELL   So. What did you find there?

ANNIE   I don't know yet.

MITCHELL   Stop looking, Annie. It's too late.

ANNIE   Why? Because I'm old?

MITCHELL   Because death *is* tapping on the inside of your
               skull. Because there's nothing you can do about
               that or anything else. All you're doing is turning
               over rocks. And there's nothing you can do with
               what you find. All you're going to get is—
               information.

ANNIE   I want information.

MITCHELL   Do you think it'll be just words? "Ecstasy"?
               "Disaster"? Words you read somewhere? Not flesh
               and bone, muscle. Not the people in your life. Just
               words? Just—paper out of your schoolteacher's
               books?

                              Pause.

ANNIE   Names. Dates. Places. That's how I learned, so
               that's how I taught. I was wrong? Fine. I was
               wrong. Paper is wrong. Fine. It's wrong. *(she tears
               pages out of a book)* She comes back to tell me
               that? That I gave marks for—spelling and neatness,
               for *paper*. While she gave marks for—*imagination*.
               She comes back sixty years later to tell me I was a
               bad teacher?

                              Pause.

MITCHELL   Yes. That's right. A bad teacher.

ANNIE   She sends the boy to tell me that?

MITCHELL   Yes, Annie. She sends the boy to tell you that.

                              Pause.

ANNIE   You're lying to me, Mitchell. *(pause)* Please don't
               lie to me. *(pause)* What is she saying?

Pause.

MITCHELL   She's saying what she's saying. Leave it alone.

ANNIE   Please, Mitchell. I'm old. I'm dying. I need it
             simple.

Pause.

MITCHELL   *(quiet, resigned)* Water. Bread. Meat. Schoolbooks.
             Houses. Hospital beds. Jobs. Land. There ain't
             enough to go around. There ain't enough, someone
             comes up short. It ain't pretty, this coming up
             short; it gets hungry and cold, and the kids can't add
             or subtract. And people like your sister. Your
             sister, Annie. Die on cold linoleum in some scruffy
             room.

             But once in a long while folks who come up short
             start making a fuss. And so you hire men like me.
             And I take care of these folks. Deport as many as
             possible. Build camps in the bush, hide people
             away, out of sight, out of mind. But one year that
             isn't enough. Men like me become soldiers.
             Bayonets. Machine guns. Whatever it takes. We
             become a private army—because there is not
             enough to go around.

             We fight the enemy on the streets of a small prairie
             city. In this fight is a city detective with a steel
             plate in his head, a veteran of the Great War. This
             detective gets a tap on his steel plate, and he is
             dead. He is dead, and the government has its martyr,
             sacrificed for you. I die beside him, Annie, without
             com-plaint or criticism, because that is my job.
             And you paid me to do this. You paid me.

ANNIE   That's just politics, Mitchell.

MITCHELL   Annie. I was clubbed to death for your....

ANNIE   Survival. Survival of the fittest.

MITCHELL   Are you fit? Or are you lucky? Are we talking
            survival? I don't think so. Survival is natural. An
            animal instinct. Aren't we talking about—your
            prosperity. Not your survival. Your comfort.
            Bought and paid for. A dumb working-class kid,
            clubbed to death by other dumb working-class kids.
            Me, Annie. Me.

ANNIE   Politics, Mitchell. Zakarchuk politics. And if that's
            all you have to say, I'm not interested.

                        Pause.

MITCHELL   Well. Annie Maud McBr....

                        His voice fades out. Pause.

            Just politics. Just me. Fighting to protect your
            house. Me. But maybe I do that because... what I
            want... is in. Maybe *politics*—is entering your
            house through the window, breaking into a place
            that *I do not belong.* Jimmying the lock on a door
            that keeps me *out.* Politics, Annie. Wanting to
            sleep under this roof, this lovely gabled roof. And
            if the only way I can sleep in a house like this—if
            the only way—is to sleep—with someone—like
            you—then I would do it. And that, Annie Maud
            McBride—*that*—is politics.

                        Pause. Silence.

            Did you get what you wanted? Every rock in the
            field? Snakes everywhere?

                        Pause.

            Well, no. Not quite every rock. There's one left.
            The bohunk's spawn.

                        Music bridge.

Act Two, Scene Six

        ZAK *rollerblades in with a pot of soup in his hand.*

ANNIE   What's this?

ZAK   Meals on wheels.

ANNIE   *(smells it)* Mushroom. Canned. I haven't even taught you how to cook. *(pause)* Who are you, boy?

ZAK   I'm Zak.

        Pause.

ANNIE   Who are you, boy?

ZAK   I'm family.

ANNIE   I have no family. Who are you?

ZAK   You know who I am. You know what I am.

        Pause.

ANNIE   Are you going to change?

ZAK   People don't change. People die.

        Pause.

ANNIE   What do we do now?

ZAK   Wait.

ANNIE   For me to die.

ZAK   For the world to turn. For history to unfold. For the new world order. We wait.

ANNIE	Two old moons. Reflecting the dim, dumb light of the other. Circling.
ZAK	Moons, Annie?
ANNIE	Cold, boy. Arctic.
ZAK	Times are tough.
MITCHELL	Ask him.
ANNIE	My sister.
ZAK	What about her?

Pause.

ANNIE	How did she die?
ZAK	Real world?
ANNIE	Real world.
ZAK	*(smiles)* Thatta girl, Annie. Pedal to the medal. No fear.

Pause. He doesn't look at her. FLO enters during the following.

(simply) You get tired of the smell. Old food. Old clothes. Old skin. Old teeth. You suffocate on old words. You choke on old dreams. She talks all the time about... how to live in the world. She stinks up the room talking about... how to live with people. She just stinks up the room.

So one morning you get up. She's already there. Like a bad report card. She's already telling you. You don't even think about it. You don't even think about it, 'cause you been dreaming about it for days and months and forever. You just get tired of the smell. So one morning you take care of the smell. And you can breathe again.

> *Pause. He looks at* ANNIE *and smiles.*

I'm really glad we don't have to air out this room, too.

> FLO *steps forward. It is 1935.*

FLO Look at them, Annie. They're beautiful.

ANNIE Those guys?

FLO Lean and hungry, like wolves.

ANNIE Hobos, Flo. Hobos come knocking on the back door, begging jam sandwiches.

FLO They don't look like bums to me. Look at that one. See him? The arms on him? He can put his shoes under my bed any time he likes.

ANNIE You're crazy.

FLO This is the only exciting thing that ever happened in Regina. If you don't count the tornado.

ANNIE You're crazy.

FLO Oh, God, I'm gonna die. *(points)* That one looks like a movie star.

ANNIE Well. Maybe John Barrymore.

FLO Douglas Fairbanks.

ANNIE William Hart.

FLO Tom Mix.

ANNIE Al Jolson.

FLO Gabby Hayes

ANNIE Buster.

FLO   Charlie.

ANNIE   *(makes a face)* Lon Chaney in *Phantom of the Opera.*

FLO   Valentino. Oh, you know what I think? I think this is Christmas morning in June. I think Santa Claus has given us a couple thousand single young boys as Christmas presents.

                ZAKARCHUK enters. FLO sees him. FLO and ZAKARCHUK start to fall in love.

FLO   I think I'm going to unwrap one of those presents. Yes, Annie girl, I am. And something's coming, something very good. Things are changing, Annie. Can you feel it in the air? Things are gonna change.

                No one moves. Except for ZAK, who punches up a tune on the CD player. The tune is loud. And it's not very pretty. And Annie is surrounded by her life.

                The lights fade to black.